Diabetic Pressure Pot Unmissable Recipes

Enjoy These Amazing Diabetic Recipes for Daily Healthy Meals

Cassandra Lane

By reading this document, the reader agrees that under no circumstances is the author responsible for any losses, direct or indirect, which are incurred as a result of the use of information contained within this document, including, but not limited to, — errors, omissions, or inaccuracies.

Table of Contents

Rosemary Lamb Chops

Servings: 4

Cooking Time: 2 Minutes /44 minutes

Ingredients:

• 1 ½ pounds lamb chops (4 small chops)

• 1 teaspoon kosher salt

• Leaves from 1 (6-inch) rosemary sprig

• 2 tablespoons avocado oil

• 1 shallot, peeled and cut in quarters

• 1 tablespoon tomato paste

• 1 cup beef broth

Directions:

1. Place the lamb chops on a cutting board. Press the salt and rosemary leaves into both sides of the chops. Let rest at room temperature for to 30 minutes.

2. Set the electric pressure cooker to Sauté/More setting. When hot, add the avocado oil.

3. Brown the lamb chops, about 2 minutes per side. (If they don't all fit in a single layer, brown them in

batches.)

4. Transfer the chops to a plate. in the pot, combine the shallot, tomato paste, and broth. Cook for about a minute, scraping up the brown bits from the bottom. Hit Cancel.

5. Add the chops and any accumulated juices back to the pot.

6. Close and lock the lid of the pressure cooker. Set the valve to sealing.

7. Cook on high pressure for 2 minutes.

8. When the cooking is complete, hit Cancel and quick release the pressure.

9. Once the pin drops, unlock and remove the lid.

10. Place the lamb chops on plates and serve immediately.

11. Nutrition info: Per serving(1 LAMB CHOP):

Calories: 233; Total Fat: 18g; Protein: 15g;

Carbohydrates: 1g; Sugars: 1; Fiber: 0g; Sodium:

450mg

Mary's Meatloaf

Servings: 6

Cooking Time: 35 Minutes

Ingredients:

• ¼ cup breadcrumbs

• ⅓ cup 2% milk

• 2 large shallots, grated on the large holes of a box grater (about ¾ cup)

• 2 large eggs, lightly beaten

• ½ teaspoon salt

• ½ teaspoon freshly ground black pepper

• 1½ pounds ground chuck steak

• 8 ounces ground sirloin

• ¼ cup Spiced Tomato Ketchup or ketchup

Directions:

1. In a large bowl, combine the breadcrumbs and milk. Let the mixture stand for 5 minutes. in a large bowl, combine the breadcrumbs and milk. Let the mixture

stand for 5 minutes. by-6-inch rectangle. Grease the foil.

2. To the breadcrumb mixture, add the shallots, eggs, salt, and pepper. Stir to combine.

3. Add the ground chuck and ground sirloin. Mix with your hands until it holds together. (At first it might seem too wet; keep mixing until it comes together.)

4. Pour 2 cups of water into the electric pressure cooker and insert a wire rack or trivet.

5. Place the meat mixture in the center of the foil and shape it into a 7-by-inch loaf. Using the foil as a sling, lower the meatloaf into the pot onto the rack. Spread the ketchup on top of the meatloaf.

6. Close and lock the lid of the pressure cooker. Set the valve to sealing.

7. Cook on high pressure for 35 minutes.

8. When the cooking is complete, hit Cancel and quick release the pressure.

9. Once the pin drops, unlock and remove the lid.

10. Check the internal temperature of the meatloaf. If it is not at least 155°F, replace the lid and cook on high pressure for an additional 5 minutes.

11. Lift the meatloaf out of the pressure cooker onto a cutting board and let it rest for 5 minutes.

12. Slice and serve.

13. Nutrition info: Per serving: Calories: 340; Total Fat: 15g; Protein: 29g; Carbohydrates: 21g; Sugars: 3g; Fiber: 1g; Sodium: 371mg

Corned Beef Stew

Servings: 2

Cooking Time: 10 Minutes

Ingredients:

• 1lb corned beef

• 1lb chopped winter vegetables

• 1 cup low sodium beef broth

• 1 cup green peas

Directions:

1. Mix all the ingredients in your Pressure Pot.

2. Cook on Stew for 10 minutes.

3. Release the pressure naturally.

4. Nutrition info: Per serving: Calories: 380;Carbs: 9 ;Sugar: 2 ;Fat: 19 ;Protein: 38 ;GL: 3

Orange Glazed Steak

Servings: 4

Cooking Time: 23 Minutes

Ingredients:

- 1 pound flank steak, cut into ¼-inch thick strips
- 1 tablespoon Yacon syrup
- 1 tablespoon arrowroot starch
- 1 tablespoon water
- 1 tablespoon olive oil
- 2 garlic cloves, minced
- ½ teaspoon fresh orange zest, grated
- ½ cup fresh orange juice
- Salt and ground black pepper, as required
- ¼ teaspoon red pepper flakes, crushed

Directions:

1. in the Pressure Pot, place oil and press "Sauté".
Then, add the steak, salt and black pepper and cook for
about 5 minutes or until browned completely.

2. Add the garlic and cook for about 1 minute.

3. Press "Cancel" and stir in the orange zest, orange juice, Yacon syrup and red pepper flakes.

4. Close the lid and place the pressure valve to "Seal" position.

5. Press "Manual" and cook under "High Pressure" for about 12 minutes.

6. Press "Cancel" and carefully allow a "Quick" release.

7. Meanwhile, in a bowl, dissolve the arrowroot starch in water.

8. Open the lid and press "Sauté".

9. Add the arrowroot starch mixture, stirring continuously.

10. Cook for about 4-5 minutes, stirring continuously.

11. Press "Cancel" and serve hot.

12. Nutrition info: Per serving: Calories: 280, Fats: 13g, Carbs:7.1g, Sugar:3.5g, Proteins: 31.9g, Sodium: 105mg

Pork Chili

Servings: 10

Cooking Time: 30 Minutes

Ingredients:

• 3 pounds boneless pork shoulder, trimmed and cut into 2-inch chunks• ¾ pound tomatoes, chopped finely

• 6 Serrano peppers, chopped roughly

• 1 medium yellow onion, chopped

• ½ cup water

• 6 garlic cloves, peeled

• 1 tablespoon dried thyme

• 1-2 tablespoons red chili powder

• 1 tablespoon ground cumin

• Salt and ground black pepper, as required

• 2 tablespoon fresh lemon juice

Directions:

1. in the pot of Pressure Pot, place all ingredients except lime juice and stir to combine.

2. Close the lid and place the pressure valve to "Seal"

position.

3. Press "Manual" and cook under "High Pressure" for about minutes.

4. Press "Cancel" and allow a "Natural" release.

5. Open the lid and with a slotted spoon, transfer the pork pieces into a bowl.

6. in the pan, stir in lime juice and with an immersion blender, blend the mixture until pureed.

7. Stir in pork and serve.

8. Nutrition info: Per serving: Calories: 215, Fats:5.2g, Carbs:4.1g, Sugar:1.6g, Proteins: 26.4g, Sodium: 106mg

Oxtail Soup

Servings: 2

Cooking Time: 35 Minutes

Ingredients:

• 1lb of prepared ox tail

• 1lb chopped Mediterranean vegetables

• 1 cup low sodium beef broth

Directions:

1. Mix all the ingredients in your Pressure Pot.

2. Cook on Stew for 35 minutes.

3. Release the pressure naturally.

4. Nutrition info: Per serving: Calories: 200;Carbs: 2 ;Sugar: 0 ;Fat: 6 ;Protein: 37 ;GL: 1

Steak in Sweet & Tangy Sauce

Servings: 4

Cooking Time: 22 Minutes

Ingredients:

• 1 pound flank steaks, trimmed and cut into ¼-inch thick strips

• ½ cup plus 1½ tablespoons water, divided

• 1 tablespoon Yacon syrup

• 1 tablespoon arrowroot starch

• 2 tablespoons fresh parsley, chopped

• Salt and ground black pepper, as required

• ½ tablespoon olive oil

• 2 garlic cloves, minced

• 2 tablespoons fresh lemon juice

Directions:

1. Season the steak with salt and black pepper lightly.

2. in the Pressure Pot, place oil and press "Sauté". Now add the steak, salt and black pepper and cook for about 5 minutes.

3. With a slotted spoon, transfer the beef into a bowl.

4. In the pot, add garlic and cook for about 1 minute.

5. Press "Cancel" and stir in the beef, ½ cup of water, lemon juice and Yacon syrup.

6. Close the lid and place the pressure valve to "Seal" position.

7. Press "Manual" and cook under "High Pressure" for about 12 minutes.

8. Press "Cancel" and carefully allow a "Quick" release.

9. Meanwhile, in a small bowl, dissolve arrowroot starch in remaining water.

10. Open the lid and press "Sauté".

11. Add the arrowroot mixture in Pressure Pot, stirring continuously.

12. Cook for about 4-5 minutes or until the desired thickness, stirring continuously.

13. Press "Cancel" and stir in parsley.

14. Serve hot.

15. Nutrition info: Per serving: Calories: 253,

Fats:11.3g, Carbs: 4g, Sugar:1.1g, Proteins: 31.8g,

Sodium: 107mg

Steak and Kidney Stew

Servings: 2

Cooking Time: 35 Minutes

Ingredients:

• 1lb diced stewing steak

• 0.5lb diced kidneys

• 1lb chopped vegetables

• 1 cup low sodium beef broth

• 0.5 cup low carb beer

Directions:

1. Mix all the ingredients in your Pressure Pot.

2. Cook on Stew for 35 minutes.

3. Release the pressure naturally.

4. Nutrition info: Per serving: Calories: 380;Carbs: 10 ;Sugar: 3 ;Fat: 12 ;Protein: ;GL: 4

Lamb Curry

Servings: 4

Cooking Time: 20 Minutes

Ingredients:

• 2 lbs. diced lamb shoulder

• 2 chopped onions

• 5 minced garlic cloves

• 1 chopped bell pepper

• 4 chopped carrots

• 15 oz. diced tomatoes

• 1 cup coconut milk

• ¼ cup water

• ¼ cup lemon juice

• 6 oz. fresh baby spinach

• 1½ tbsps. curry powder

• 1 tsp. ground ginger

• ½ tsp. kosher salt

• ¼ tsp. black pepper

• ¼ tsp. cayenne pepper

Directions:

1. Press the "Sauté" function on your Pressure Pot and sear the lamb on all sides. Set side.

2. Discard the rendered fat, leaving 1 tablespoon in the Pressure Pot.

3. Add the vegetables and cook for about 5-7 minutes until softened.

4. Add in the garlic, ginger, curry powder, salt, black pepper, and cayenne pepper (if using). Stir until all the spices have bloomed.

5. Return the seared lamb to the pot and stir well to coat completely in the sautéed vegetables and spices.

6. Pour in the tomatoes along with their juices. Stir.

7. Add the coconut milk, with ¼ cup water, and gently stir.

8. Cover, setting the pressure release valve to "Sealing", and cook on "Manual, High Pressure" for 20 minutes.

9. Once done, release the pressure naturally for 10 minutes and then release any remaining pressure.

10. Add the baby spinach and let it cook in the residual heat for about 5-minutes, stirring well.

11. Stir in the lemon juice and serve garnished with cilantro or mint.

12. Nutrition info: Calories 273, Carbs 17g, Fat 13 g, Protein 22g, Potassium (K) 936 mg, Sodium (Na) 326 mg

Balsamic Beef Pot Roast

Servings: 3

Cooking Time: 50 Minutes

Ingredients:

- 3 pounds chuck roast, boneless
- 1/2 cup chopped white onion
- 1 teaspoon garlic powder
- 1 tablespoon salt
- 1 teaspoon black ground pepper
- 1/4 teaspoon xanthan gum
- 1/4 cup balsamic vinegar
- 1 tablespoon olive oil
- 2 cups beef broth
- 2 tablespoons chopped parsley

Directions:

1. Stir together garlic, salt, and black pepper and rub this mixture on all sides of roast until evenly coated.

2. Plugin Pressure Pot, insert the inner pot, press sauté/simmer button, add oil and when hot, add

seasoned roast and cook for 4 minutes per side or until nicely golden brown.

3. Add remaining ingredients except for xanthan gum and parsley, stir until mixed and press the cancel button.

4. Shut the Pressure Pot with its lid, turn the pressure knob to seal the pot, press the „manual" button, then press the „timer" to set the cooking time to 30 minutes and cook at high pressure, Pressure Pot will take 5 minutes or more for building its inner pressure.

5. When the timer beeps, press „cancel" button and do natural pressure release for 10 minutes and then do quick pressure release until pressure nob drops down.

6. Open the Pressure Pot, transfer roast to a plate and break into bite-size pieces.

7. Press the „sauté/simmer" button, add xanthan gum into the Pressure Pot and cook for 3 to 5 minutes or until cooking sauce is reduced by half.

8. Return beef into the Pressure Pot, stir until just

mixed and press the cancel button.

9. Garnish beef with parsley and serve.

10. Nutrition info: Calories: 322 Cal, Carbs: 4 g, Fat: 20 g, Protein: 32 g, Fiber: 4 g.

Mustard Pork Chops

Servings: 4

Cooking Time: 25 Minutes

Ingredients:

• 4 pork chops, each about 1-inch thick

• 2 tablespoons salt

• 1 tablespoon ground black pepper

• 2 tablespoons honey

• 15-ounce mustard barbecue sauce, unsweetened

• 1 cup water

Directions:

1. Plugin Pressure Pot, insert the inner pot, add honey, barbecue sauce and water and whisk until mixed.

2. Season pork chops with salt and black pepper, then add to the Pressure Pot, shut the Pressure Pot with its lid and turn the pressure knob to seal the pot.

3. Press the „manual" button, then press the „timer" to set the cooking time to 15 minutes and cook at high pressure, Pressure Pot will take 5 minutes or more for

building its inner pressure.

4. When the timer beeps, press „cancel" button and do quick pressure release until pressure nob drops down.

5. Open the Pressure Pot, press the „sauté/simmer" button and cook for minutes or until cooking sauce in Pressure Pot is reduce by half.

6. Press the cancel button, transfer pork chops to serving plates and ladle cooking sauce over it.

7. Serve straight away.

8. Nutrition info: Calories: 165 Cal, Carbs: 9 g, Fat: 5 g, Protein: 19 g, Fiber: 0 g.

Roast Beef

Servings: 2

Cooking Time: 60 Minutes

Ingredients:

• 1lb trimmed, tied beef joint

• 1lb cubed winter vegetables

• 1 cup low sodium beef broth

• 1 cup gravy

Directions:

1. Mix the broth and gravy.

2. Place the beef in your Pressure Pot.

3. Pour the broth and gravy on top.

4. Cook on Stew for 60 minutes.

5. Release the pressure naturally.

6. Nutrition info: Per serving: Calories: 275;Carbs: 5 ;Sugar: 0 ;Fat: 7 ;Protein: 49 ;GL: 2

Mary's Sunday Pot Roast

Servings: 10

Cooking Time: 1 Hour 30 Minutes

Ingredients:

• 1 (3- to 4-pound) beef rump roast

• 2 teaspoons kosher salt, divided

• 2 tablespoons avocado oil

• 1 large onion, coarsely chopped (about 1½ cups)

• 4 large carrots, each cut into 4 pieces

• 1 tablespoon minced garlic

• 3 cups low-sodium beef broth

• 1 teaspoon freshly ground black pepper

• 1 tablespoon dried parsley

• 2 tablespoons all-purpose flour

Directions:

1. Rub the roast all over with teaspoon of the salt.

2. Set the electric pressure cooker to the Sauté setting. When the pot is hot, pour in the avocado oil.

3. Carefully place the roast in the pot and sear it for 6

to 9 minutes on each side. (You want a dark caramelized crust.) Hit Cancel.

4. Transfer the roast from the pot to a plate.

5. in order, put the onion, carrots, and garlic in the pot. Place the roast on top of the vegetables along with any juices that accumulated on the plate.

6. in a medium bowl, whisk together the broth, remaining 1 teaspoon of salt, pepper, and parsley. Pour the broth mixture over the roast.

7. Close and lock the lid of the pressure cooker. Set the valve to sealing.

8. Cook on high pressure for 1 hour and 30 minutes.

9. When the cooking is complete, hit Cancel and allow the pressure to release naturally.

10. Once the pin drops, unlock and remove the lid.

11. Using large, slotted spoons, transfer the roast and vegetables to a serving platter while you make the gravy.

12. Using a large spoon or fat separator, remove the fat

from the juices in the pot. Set the electric pressure cooker to the Sauté setting and bring the liquid to a boil.

13. in a small bowl, whisk together the flour and 4 tablespoons of water to make a slurry. Pour the slurry into the pot, whisking occasionally, until the gravy is the thickness you like. Season with salt and pepper, if necessary.

14. Serve the meat and carrots with the gravy.

15. Nutrition info: Per serving: Calories: 245; Total Fat: 10g; Protein: 33g; Carbohydrates: 6g; Sugars: 2g; Fiber: 1g; Sodium: 397mg

Sweet and Sour Pork Chops

Servings: 4

Cooking Time: 1 Minute

Ingredients:

For the sauce

• 3 tablespoons Spiced Tomato Ketchup or store-
bought ketchup

• 1 tablespoon Worcestershire sauce

• 1 teaspoon yellow mustard

• ½ teaspoon freshly squeezed lemon juice

• Few drops hot pepper sauce (optional)

For the pork chops

• 4 (¾-inch-thick) rib pork chops

• Kosher salt

• Freshly ground black pepper

• 2 tablespoons avocado oil, divided

• 1 (8-ounce) can pineapple chunks in juice

• 2 tablespoons cornstarch

• 1 medium green bell pepper, cut into thin strips

Directions:

1. To make the sauce

2. in a cup liquid measuring cup or small bowl, mix together the ketchup, Worcestershire sauce, mustard, lemon juice, and hot pepper sauce (if using).

3. To make the pork chops

4. Set the electric pressure cooker to the Sauté setting. Sprinkle both sides of pork chops with salt and pepper and use a meat tenderizing mallet to pound both sides. (If you don't have a mallet, you can use a rolling pin, or try my grandpa's trick of using the edge of a small plate.) When the pot is hot, pour in 1 tablespoon of avocado oil.

5. Add 2 pork chops to the pot in a single layer and brown for 2 to 3 minutes per side. Transfer the pork chops to a plate. Repeat with the remaining avocado oil and pork chops. Hit Cancel.

6. Drain the pineapple juice from the can into a 2-cup liquid measuring cup. Add enough water so that you

have 1 cup of liquid. Pour this into the pot and scrape up any browned bits that are stuck to the bottom. Set the pineapple chunks aside.

7. Return the pork chops to the pot (overlapping them is fine); pour some of the sauce mixture on top of each one.

8. Close and lock the lid of the pressure cooker. Set the valve to sealing.

9. Cook on high pressure for 1 minute.

10. When the cooking is complete, allow the pressure to release naturally for minutes, then quick release any remaining pressure. Hit Cancel.

11. Once the pin drops, unlock and remove the lid.

12. Remove the pork chops from the pot. Hit Sauté.

13. in a small bowl, mix together the cornstarch and 3 tablespoons of cold water to make a slurry. Add it to the pot and cook, stirring frequently, for a few minutes, until the mixture begins to thicken.

14. Add the reserved pineapple and green pepper to the

pot. Cook, stirring occasionally, for about 5 minutes or until the green pepper softens. Hit Cancel. Return the pork chops to the pot and coat with sauce.

15. Place the pork chops on serving plates, top with sauce, and serve.

16. Nutrition info: Per serving: Calories: 407; Total Fat: 17g; Protein: 45g; Carbohydrates: ; Sugars: 11g; Fiber: 1g; Sodium: 416mg

Lamb and Mushroom Stew

Servings: 2

Cooking Time: 35 Minutes

Ingredients:

- 1lb diced lamb

- 1lb chopped vegetables

- 1 cup mushrooms

- 1 cup mushroom soup

- 1tbsp black pepper

Directions:

1. Mix all the ingredients in your Pressure Pot.

2. Cook on Stew for 35 minutes.

3. Release the pressure naturally.

4. Nutrition info: Per serving: Calories: 3;Carbs: 3 ;Sugar: 0 ;Fat: 19 ;Protein: 45 ;GL: 1

Beef Pot Roast

Servings: 5

Cooking Time: 45 Minutes

Ingredients:

- 3 tsp. extra-virgin olive oil, divided
- 2 lbs. beef chuck roast
- 4 quartered red potatoes
- 4 sliced carrots
- 2 quartered yellow onions
- 2 dried bay leaves
- 2 cups low-sodium beef broth
- 2 tbsps. Worcestershire sauce
- 1 tbsp. cider vinegar
- 1 tbsp. cornstarch
- 1 tbsp. tomato paste
- 1 tbsp. minced garlic
- 1 tbsp. smoked paprika
- 1 tsp. black pepper

- ½ tsp. kosher salt

- ¼ tsp. cayenne pepper

Directions:

1. Select the "Sauté" function on your Pressure Pot and heat 2 teaspoons of oil.

2. Add the meat and sear on all sides, about 3 minutes per side. Set aside for now.

3. Add the remaining teaspoon of oil to the pot.

4. Add the bay leaves, tomato paste, garlic, black pepper, paprika, salt and cayenne pepper to the pot, and stir cooking for 1 minute.

5. Stir in the broth and Worcestershire sauce, deglazing the pot. Add the potatoes and carrots.

6. Place the roast on top of the vegetables and scatter the onions on top.

7. Close and seal the lid, setting the pressure release valve to "Sealing."

8. Cook on "Manual, High Pressure" setting for 45 minutes.

9. Once done, release the pressure manually and uncover the beef.

10. Transfer the beef and vegetables to a platter and gently shred the meat.

11. Skim the fat off the cooking liquid in the pot.

12. Transfer ¼ cup of the cooking juices to a small bowl and set aside.

13.Return the pot to the "Sauté" function and bring the remaining liquid to a simmer.

14. Whisk the cornstarch and reserved ¼ cup of liquid, and then add to the pot.

15. Simmer until the sauce thickens, about 5 to 8 minutes, and then stir in the vinegar.

16. Serve the sauce over the shredded beef and vegetables.

17. Nutrition info: Calories 296, Carbs 24g, Fat 8 g, Protein 29g, Potassium (K) 878 mg, Sodium (Na) 508 mg

Shredded Beef

Servings: 2

Cooking Time: 35 Minutes

Ingredients:

- 1.5lb lean steak

- 1 cup low sodium gravy

- 2tbsp mixed spices

Directions:

1. Mix all the ingredients in your Pressure Pot.

2. Cook on Stew for 35 minutes.

3. Release the pressure naturally.

4. Shred the beef.

5. Nutrition info: Per serving: Calories: 200;Carbs: 2 ;Sugar: 0 ;Fat: ;Protein: 48 ;GL: 1

Lamb Shoulder

Servings: 6

Cooking Time: 1 Hr. 30 Minutes

Ingredients:

- 2 tsp. good olive oil

- 4 lbs. bone-in lamb shoulder

- 2 cups low-sodium beef or chicken stock

- 1 sprig fresh rosemary

- 6 chopped anchovies

- 1 tsp. garlic purée

- 1 tsp. dried oregano

- 1 1/2 tsps. Kosher salt

Directions:

1. Select the "Sauté" function on your Pressure Pot and add oil.

2. Once hot, add the lamb shoulder and sear until nicely browned. Set aside for now.

3. Add the chicken stock to deglaze the bottom of the pan and then stir in the anchovies and garlic.

4. Return the lamb to the Pressure Pot insert, sprinkle with salt and oregano, and then add the rosemary sprig.

5. Cover and seal the Pressure Pot, turning the pressure valve to "Sealing."

6. Cook on the "Manual, High Pressure" setting for 1½ hours.

7. Once done, allow for a 15-minute natural pressure release and then do a quick pressure release to release any remaining steam.

8. Slice and serve with your favorite side.

9. Nutrition info: Calories 300, Carbs 3g, Fat 12 g, Protein 40g, Potassium (K) 646 mg, Sodium (Na) 250 mg

Lamb and Chickpea Stew

Servings: 8

Cooking Time: 45 Minutes

Ingredients:

- 1 tbsp. cooking oil
- 2 lbs. cubed lamb shoulder
- 2 chopped white onions
- 4 chopped garlic cloves.
- 28 oz. diced tomatoes
- ¾ cup low-salt chicken broth
- 1 cinnamon stick
- ½ cup dried chickpeas
- 1 tbsp. ground coriander
- 1 tbsp. ground cumin
- 1 tsp. black pepper
- ½ tsp. cayenne pepper
- ¼ tsp. ground cloves
- ¼ tsp. sea salt

To Serve:

- Fresh cilantro

- Plain yogurt

Directions:

1. Mix together the coriander, cumin, cayenne pepper, cloves, black pepper, and salt in a medium bowl.

2. Add the lamb and toss well to coat.

3. Select the "Sauté" function on the Pressure Pot, add the oil and warm up the pot.

4. Sauté the onions and garlic about 5 minutes until softened, and then push aside the onions and return the lamb, sautéing until browned.

5. Stir in the broth, tomatoes, cinnamon, and chickpeas.

6. Close and seal the Pressure Pot lid.

7. Set the pressure release valve to "Sealing", and then press the "Cancel" button to stop the "Sauté" function.

8. Select the "Manual, High Pressure" setting and cook for 45 minutes.

9. Once the cook cycle is up, press the "Cancel" button

and allow the pressure to release naturally, about 30 minutes.

10. Remove the lid, discard the cinnamon and then taste and adjust the seasonings.

11. Serve garnished with fresh cilantro and yogurt for garnish.

12. This flavorful lamb will keep for up to 4 days refrigerated.

13. Nutrition info: Calories 240, Carbs 15g, Fat 10 g, Protein 24g, Potassium (K) 685.9 mg, Sodium (Na) 300 mg

Tangy Pulled Beef

Servings: 10

Cooking Time: 1 Hour 20 Minutes

Ingredients:

• 3 pounds beef chuck roast, trimmed and cut into large chunks• 1 large yellow onion, sliced

• 3-4 green chilies, chopped

• ¾ cup water

• 6 garlic cloves, minced

• ¼ cup fresh lime juice

• 1 tablespoon dried oregano

• Salt and ground black pepper, as required

Directions:

1. in the pot of Pressure Pot, place all ingredients and stir to combine.

2. Close the lid and place the pressure valve to "Seal" position.

3. Press "Manual" and cook under "High Pressure" for about 1 hour.

4. Press "Cancel" and allow a "Natural" release.

5. Open the lid and place the roast onto a plate.

6. with 2 forks, shred the meat and return into Pressure Pot.

7. Now, press "Sauté" and cook for about 15-20 minutes or until desired doneness of sauce.

8. Press "Cancel" and serve hot.

9. Nutrition info: Per serving: Calories: 480, Fats: 35g, Carbs:2.4g, Sugar: 0.7g, Proteins: 36.5g, Sodium: 104mg

Beef with Bell Peppers

Servings: 5

Cooking Time: 33 Minutes

Ingredients:

• 1 pound boneless beef, trimmed and cut into thin strips

• 3 cups tomatoes, chopped finely

• 3 large bell peppers, seeded and cut into ½-inch thick strips

• 1 large onion, cut into ½-inch thick strips

• 1 cup water

• 1 tablespoon olive oil

• Salt and ground black pepper, as required

• 2 garlic cloves, minced

• 1 teaspoon dried thyme, crushed

Directions:

1. in the Pressure Pot, place oil and press "Sauté". Then, add the beef, salt and black pepper and cook for about 5-6 minutes or until browned completely

2. with a slotted spoon, transfer the beef into a bowl.

3. in the pot, add the tomatoes, garlic, thyme, salt and black pepper and cook for about 1-2 minutes.

4. Press "Cancel" and stir in the beef, onion, bell peppers and water.

5. Close the lid and place the pressure valve to "Seal" position.

6. Press "Manual" and cook under "High Pressure" for about 25 minutes.

7. Press "Cancel" and carefully allow a "Quick" release.

8. Open the lid and serve hot.

9. Nutrition info: Per serving: Calories: 27 Fats: 17g, Carbs:12.9g, Sugar: 7g, Proteins: 19.5g, Sodium: 88mg

Chili Lime Steak Bowl

Servings: 6

Cooking Time: 22 Minutes

Ingredients:

- 2 pounds steaks, cut into strips
- 1 teaspoon minced garlic
- ½ teaspoon salt
- ½ teaspoon ground black pepper
- ½ teaspoon red chili powder
- 1 teaspoon hot sauce
- 2 teaspoons lime juice
- 1 tablespoon olive oil
- 1 tablespoon water
- 3 mediums avocado, pitted and flesh diced

Directions:

1. Plugin Pressure Pot, insert the inner pot, press sauté/simmer button, add oil and when hot, add garlic and cook for minute or until fragrant.

2. Then add remaining ingredients except for avocado

and stir until mixed.

3. Press the cancel button, shut the Pressure Pot with its lid and turn the pressure knob to seal the pot.

4. Press the „manual" button, then press the „timer" to set the cooking time to 10 minutes and cook at high pressure, Pressure Pot will take 5 minutes or more for building its inner pressure.

5. When the timer beeps, press „cancel" button and do quick pressure release until pressure nob drops down.

6. Open the Pressure Pot, press the „sauté/simmer" button and cook for 5 minutes or until cooking sauce is reduce by half.

7. Evenly divide steaks between serving plates and serve with avocado.

8. Nutrition info: Calories: 437 Cal, Carbs: 15.1 g, Fat: 26.2 g, Protein: 35.4 g, Fiber: 0 g.

Pork Roast

Servings: 6

Cooking Time: 50 Minutes

Ingredients:

- 2 pounds pork roast, fat trimmed
- 1 teaspoon garlic powder
- 2 teaspoons salt
- 1/2 teaspoon ground black pepper
- 1 teaspoon dried thyme
- 1 teaspoon dried rosemary
- 1 tablespoon oil
- 2 cups chicken broth

Directions:

1. Stir together garlic, salt, black pepper, thyme, and rosemary and sprinkle this mixture on all sides of pork or until evenly coated.

2. Plugin Pressure Pot, insert the inner pot, press the „sauté/simmer" button, add 1 tablespoon oil and when hot, add seasoned pork and cook for 4 minutes per

side.

3. When done, transfer pork to a plate, then pour in chicken broth and stir well to remove browned bits from the bottom of the Pressure Pot.

4. Press the cancel button, insert trivet stand, place pork on it, then shut the Pressure Pot with its lid and turn the pressure knob to seal the pot.

5. Press the „meat/stew" button, then press the „timer" to set the cooking time to 30 minutes and cook at high pressure, Pressure Pot will take minutes or more for building its inner pressure.

6. When the timer beeps, press „cancel" button and do natural pressure release for 10 minutes and then do quick pressure release until pressure nob drops down.

7. Open the Pressure Pot, transfer pork to a cutting board and let rest for 10 minutes.

8. Cut pork into even slices and serve.

9. Nutrition info: Calories: 478 Cal, Carbs: 5 g, Fat: 18.1 g, Protein: 66.1 g, Fiber:2.7 g.

Pork Carnitas

Servings: 6

Cooking Time: 50 Minutes

Ingredients:

• 4 pounds boneless pork shoulder, cut into 3-inch

pieces

• 3 teaspoons minced garlic

• 1 1/2 teaspoons salt

• 1/2 teaspoon ground black pepper

• 2 teaspoons red chili powder

• 2 teaspoons dried oregano

• 1 1/2 teaspoons ground cumin

• 1/4 cup lime juice, fresh

• 1 tablespoon olive oil

• 1/2 cup orange juice, fresh

• 12-ounce beef broth

• Tortillas for serving

Directions:

1. Plugin Pressure Pot, insert the inner pot, press

sauté/simmer button, add oil and when hot, add pork pieces in a single layer and cook for 3 to 4 minutes per side or until nicely browned.2. Cook remaining pieces in the same manner, then return browned pork pieces into the instant.

pot and add remaining ingredients.

3. Press the cancel button, shut the Pressure Pot with its lid and turn the pressure knob to seal the

pot.

4. Press the „manual" button, then press the „timer" to set the cooking time to 30 minutes and

cook at high pressure, Pressure Pot will take 5 minutes or more for building its inner pressure.5. When the timer beeps, press „cancel" button and do quick pressure release until pressure nob

drops down.

6. Open the Pressure Pot, shred pork with two forks and stir until mixed.

7. Serve pork with tortillas.

8. Nutrition info: Calories: 31Cal, Carbs: 24 g, Fat: 12 g, Protein: 32 g, Fiber: 4 g.

Beef Offal Stew

Servings: 2

Cooking Time: 35 Minutes

Ingredients:

- 0.5lb diced ox heart

- 0.5lb diced kidney

- 0.5lb cured, diced ox tongue

- 1lb chopped vegetables

- 1 cup low sodium beef broth

Directions:

1. Mix all the ingredients in your Pressure Pot.

2. Cook on Stew for 35 minutes.

3. Release the pressure naturally.

4. Nutrition info: Per serving: Calories: 360;Carbs: 8 ;Sugar: 1 ;Fat: 20 ;Protein: ;GL: 3

Slow Cooked Lamb

Servings: 2

Cooking Time: 35 Minutes

Ingredients:

- 1lb diced lean lamb

- 1 quartered onion

- 2 chopped carrots

- 1 cup low sodium broth

- 0.5 cup mint sauce

Directions:

1. Place the lamb in your Pressure Pot.

2. Place the onion and carrots around it.

3. Pour the sauce and broth over it.

4. Cook on Stew for 35 minutes.

5. Release the pressure naturally.

6. Nutrition info: Per serving: Calories: 400;Carbs: 14 ;Sugar: 4 ;Fat: 20 ;Protein: 37 ;GL: 6

Herbed Leg of Lamb

Servings: 10

Cooking Time: 1 Hour 25 Minutes

Ingredients:

- 1 (4-pound) bone-in leg of lamb, trimmed
- 1 large yellow onion, sliced thinly
- 1½ cups low-sodium chicken broth
- 6 fresh thyme sprigs
- 3 fresh rosemary sprigs
- Ground black pepper, as required
- 1 tablespoon olive oil
- 2 tablespoons fresh lemon juice
- 6 garlic cloves, crushed

Directions:

1. In the Pressure Pot, place oil and press "Sauté". Now add the leg of lamb and sear for about 4 minutes per side or until browned completely.

2. Transfer the leg of lamb onto a large plate.

3. in the pot add onion and cook for about minutes.

4. Add a little broth and cook for about 2 minutes, scraping the brown bits from bottom.

5. Press "Cancel" and stir in the cooked leg of lamb and remaining ingredients.

6. Close the lid and place the pressure valve to "Seal" position.

7. Press "Manual" and cook under "High Pressure" for about minutes.

8. Press "Cancel" and allow a "Natural" release.

9. Open the lid and with tongs, transfer the leg of lamb onto a cutting board.

10. With a strainer, strain the pan liquid into a bowl, discarding the solids.

11. Cut the leg of lamb into desired sized slices.

12. Pour strained liquid over lamb slices and serve.

13. Nutrition info: Per serving: Calories: 443, Fats: 32g, Carbs:2.5g, Sugar: 0.7g, Proteins: 32.7g, Sodium: 117mg

Chickpea Soup

Servings: 2

Cooking Time: 35 Minutes

Ingredients:

- 1lb cooked chickpeas

- 1lb chopped vegetables

- 1 cup low sodium vegetable broth

- 2tbsp mixed herbs

Directions:

1. Mix all the ingredients in your Pressure Pot.

2. Cook on Stew for 35 minutes.

3. Release the pressure naturally.

4. Nutrition info: Per serving: Calories: 310;Carbs: 20 ;Sugar: 3 ;Fat: 5 ;Protein: 27 ;GL: 5

Meatless Ball Soup

Servings: 2

Cooking Time: 15 Minutes

Ingredients:

- 1lb minced tofu

- 0.5lb chopped vegetables

- 2 cups low sodium vegetable broth

- 1tbsp almond flour

- salt and pepper

Directions:

1. Mix the tofu, flour, salt and pepper.

2. Form the meatballs.

3. Place all the ingredients in your Pressure Pot.

4. Cook on Stew for 15 minutes.

5. Release the pressure naturally.

6. Nutrition info: Per serving: Calories: 240;Carbs: 9 ;Sugar: 3 ;Fat: 10 ;Protein: 35 ;GL: 5

Tofu Curry

Servings: 2

Cooking Time: 20 Minutes

Ingredients:

• 2 cups cubed extra firm tofu

• 2 cups mixed stir fry vegetables

• 0.5 cup soy yogurt

• 3tbsp curry paste

• 1tbsp oil or ghee

Directions:

1. Set the Pressure Pot to sauté and add the oil and curry paste.

2. When the onion is soft, add the remaining ingredients except the yogurt and seal.

3. Cook on Stew for 20 minutes.

4. Release the pressure naturally and serve with a scoop of soy yogurt.

5. Nutrition info: Per serving: Calories: 300;Carbs: 9 ;Sugar: 4 ;Fat: 14 ;Protein: 42 ;GL: 7

Squash Medley

Servings: 2

Cooking Time: 20 Minutes.

Ingredients:

• 2lbs mixed squash

• 0.5 cup mixed veg

• 1 cup vegetable stock

• 2tbsp olive oil

• 2tbsp mixed herbs

Directions:

1. Put the squash in the steamer basket and add the stock into the Pressure Pot.

2. Steam the squash in your Pressure Pot for 10 minutes.

3. Depressurize and pour away the remaining stock.

4. Set to sauté and add the oil and remaining ingredients.

5. Cook until a light crust forms.

6. Nutrition info: Per serving: Calories: 100;Carbs: 10 ;Sugar: 3 ;Fat: ;Protein: 5 ;GL: 20

Fake-on Stew

Servings: 2

Cooking Time: 25 Minutes

Ingredients:

• 0.5lb soy bacon

• 1lb chopped vegetables

• 1 cup low sodium vegetable broth

• 1tbsp nutritional yeast

Directions:

1. Mix all the ingredients in your Pressure Pot.

2. Cook on Stew for minutes.

3. Release the pressure naturally.

4. Nutrition info: Per serving: Calories: 200;Carbs: 12 ;Sugar: 3 ;Fat: 7 ;Protein: ;GL: 5

Chili sin Carne

Servings: 2

Cooking Time: 35 Minutes

Ingredients:

• 3 cups mixed cooked beans

• 2 cups chopped tomatoes

• 1tbsp yeast extract

• 2 squares very dark chocolate

• 1tbsp red chili flakes

Directions:

1. Mix all the ingredients in your Pressure Pot.

2. Cook on Beans for 35 minutes.

3. Release the pressure naturally.

4. Nutrition info: Per serving: Calories: 2;Carbs: 20 ;Sugar: 5 ;Fat: 3 ;Protein: 36 ;GL: 11

Kidney Bean Stew

Servings: 2

Cooking Time: 15 Minutes

Ingredients:

• 1 lb. cooked kidney beans

• 1 cup tomato passata

• 1 cup low sodium beef broth

• 3 tbsps. Italian herbs

Directions:

1. Mix all the ingredients in your Pressure Pot, cook on Stew for minutes.

2. Release the pressure naturally and serve.

3. Nutrition info: Calories 270, Carbs 16g, Fat 10g, Protein 2, Potassium (K) 663.5 mg, Sodium (Na) 641.2 mg

Fried Tofu Hotpot

Servings: 2

Cooking Time: 15 Minutes

Ingredients:

• 0.5lb fried tofu

• 1lb chopped Chinese vegetable mix

• 1 cup low sodium vegetable broth

• 2tbsp 5 spice seasoning

• 1tbsp smoked paprika

Directions:

1. Mix all the ingredients in your Pressure Pot.

2. Cook on Stew for 15 minutes.

3. Release the pressure naturally.

4. Nutrition info: Per serving: Calories: 320;Carbs: 11 ;Sugar: 3 ;Fat: 23 ;Protein: ;GL: 6

Seitan Roast

Servings: 2

Cooking Time: 35 Minutes

Ingredients:

- 1lb seitan roulade
- 1lb chopped winter vegetables
- 1 cup low sodium vegetable broth
- 4tbsp roast rub

Directions:

1. Rub the roast rub into your roulade.

2. Place the roulade and vegetables in your Pressure Pot.

3. Add the broth. Seal.

4. Cook on Stew for 35 minutes.

5. Release the pressure naturally.

6. Nutrition info: Per serving: Calories: 2;Carbs: 9 ;Sugar: 2 ;Fat: 2 ;Protein: 49 ;GL: 4

Eggplant Curry

Servings: 2

Cooking Time: 20 Minutes

Ingredients:

- 2-3 cups chopped eggplant
- 1 thinly sliced onion
- 1 cup coconut milk
- 3tbsp curry paste
- 1tbsp oil or ghee

Directions:

1. Set the Pressure Pot to sauté and add the onion, oil, and curry paste.

2. When the onion is soft, add the remaining ingredients and seal.

3. Cook on Stew for 20 minutes. Release the pressure naturally.

4. Nutrition info: Per serving: Calories: 350;Carbs: 15 ;Sugar: 3 ;Fat: 25 ;Protein: 11 ;GL: 10

Lentil and Chickpea Curry

Servings: 2

Cooking Time: 20 Minutes

Ingredients:

• 2 cups dry lentils and chickpeas

• 1 thinly sliced onion

• 1 cup chopped tomato

• 3 tbsps. curry paste

• 1 tbsp. oil or ghee

Directions:

1. Set the Pressure Pot to sauté and add the onion, oil, and curry paste.

2. When the onion is soft, add the remaining ingredients and seal.

3. Cook on Stew for 20 minutes.

4. Release the pressure naturally and serve.

5. Nutrition info: Calories 360, Carbs 26g, Fat 19g, Protein 23g, Potassium (K) 866.mg, Sodium (Na) 964.4mg

Steamed Asparagus

Servings: 4

Cooking Time: 2 Minutes

Ingredients:

• 1 lb. fresh asparagus, rinsed and tough ends trimmed

• 1 cup water

Directions:

1. Place the asparagus into a wire steamer rack and set it inside your Pressure Pot.

2. Add water to the pot. Close and seal the lid, turning the steam release valve to the "Sealing" position.

3. Select the "Steam" function to cook on high pressure for 2 minutes.

4. Once done, do a quick pressure release of the steam.

5. Lift the wire steamer basket out of the pot and place the asparagus onto a serving plate.

6. Season as desired and serve.

7. Nutrition info: Calories 22, Carbs 4g, Fat 0 g, Protein 2g, Potassium (K) 229 mg, Sodium (Na) 5 mg

Cabbage Soup

Servings: 2

Cooking Time: 10 Minutes

Ingredients:

• 2 cups finely shredded savoy cabbage

• 1 cup finely shredded red cabbage

• 1 cup chopped scallions

• 2 cups vegetable stock

• salt and pepper

Directions:

1. Mix all the ingredients in your Pressure Pot.

2. Cook on Stew for 10 minutes.

3. Depressurize naturally and blend.

4. Nutrition info: Per serving: Calories: 12;Carbs: 2 ;Sugar: 0 ;Fat: 0 ;Protein: 1 ;GL: 1

Lentil and Eggplant Stew

Servings: 2

Cooking Time: 35 Minutes

Ingredients:

- 1lb eggplant

- 1lb dry lentils

- 1 cup chopped vegetables

- 1 cup low sodium vegetable broth

Directions:

1. Mix all the ingredients in your Pressure Pot.

2. Cook on Stew for 35 minutes.

3. Release the pressure naturally.

4. Nutrition info: Per serving: Calories: 310;Carbs: 22 ;Sugar: 6 ;Fat: 10 ;Protein: 32 ;GL: 16

Mango Tofu Curry

Servings: 2

Cooking Time: 35 Minutes

Ingredients:

• 1lb cubed extra firm tofu

• 1lb chopped vegetables

• 1 cup low carb mango sauce

• 1 cup vegetable broth

• 2tbsp curry paste

Directions:

1. Mix all the ingredients in your Pressure Pot.

2. Cook on Stew for 35 minutes.

3. Release the pressure naturally.

4. Nutrition info: Per serving: Calories: 310;Carbs: 20 ;Sugar: 9 ;Fat: ;Protein: 37 ;GL: 19

Split Pea Stew

Servings: 2

Cooking Time: 35 Minutes

Ingredients:

• 1 cup dry split peas

• 1 lb. chopped vegetables

• 1 cup mushroom soup

• 2 tbsps. old bay seasoning

Directions:

1. Mix all the ingredients in your Pressure Pot, cook on Beans for 35 minutes.

2. Release the pressure naturally.

3. Nutrition info: Calories 0, Carbs 7g, Fat 2g, Protein 24g, Potassium (K) 63.2 mg, Sodium (Na) 797.7 mg

Tomato Eggs

Servings: 2

Cooking Time: 7 Minutes

Ingredients:

• 4oz egg whites

• 2tbsp milk

• zero calorie spray

• 0.5 cup chopped cherry tomatoes

• 0.5 cup chopped bell peppers, mixed colors

Directions:

1. Spray a heat-proof bowl that fits in your Pressure Pot with nonstick spray.

2. Whisk together the eggs, milk, and add a pinch of salt.

3. Pour into the bowl. Add the vegetables.

4. Place the bowl in your steamer basket.

5. Pour 1 cup of water into your Pressure Pot.

6. Lower the basket into your Pressure Pot.

7. Seal and cook on low pressure for minutes.

Depressurize quickly.

8. Stir well and allow to rest, it will finish cooking in its own heat.

Pea and Mint Soup

Servings: 2

Cooking Time: 35 Minutes

Ingredients:

• 1lb green peas

• 2 cups low sodium vegetable broth

• 3tbsp mint sauce

Directions:

1. Mix all the ingredients in your Pressure Pot.

2. Cook on Stew for 35 minutes.

3. Release the pressure naturally.

4. Blend into a rough soup.

5. Nutrition info: Per serving: Calories: 130;Carbs: 17 ;Sugar: 4 ;Fat: ;Protein: 19 ;GL: 11

Seitan Curry

Servings: 2

Cooking Time: 20 Minutes

Ingredients:

- 0.5lb seitan
- 1 thinly sliced onion
- 1 cup chopped tomato
- 3tbsp curry paste
- 1tbsp oil or ghee

Directions:

1. Set the Pressure Pot to sauté and add the onion, oil, and curry paste.

2. When the onion is soft, add the remaining ingredients and seal.

3. Cook on Stew for 20 minutes.

4. Release the pressure naturally.

5. Nutrition info: Per serving: Calories: 240;Carbs: 19 ;Sugar: 4 ;Fat: 10 ;Protein: 32 ;GL: 10

Scotch Eggs

Servings: 4

Cooking Time: 16 Minutes

Ingredients:

• 4 large eggs

• 1 pound lean ground beef

• 1 tablespoon olive oil

• Salt and ground black pepper, as required

Directions:

1. Arrange a steamer basket in the Pressure Pot and pour cup of water.

2. Place eggs into the steamer basket.

3. Close the lid and place the pressure valve to "Seal" position.

4. Press "Manual" and cook under "High Pressure" for about 6 minutes.

5. Press "Cancel" and carefully allow a "Quick" release.

6. Open the lid and transfer eggs into a bowl of cold water to cool completely.

7. After cooling, peel the eggs.

8. In a bowl, add the beef, salt and black pepper and mix well.

9. Divide the beef into 4 equal-sized portions.

10. Flat each portion into an oval-shaped patty.

11. Place 1 egg in the middle of each patty and gently, mold the meat around egg.

12. Remove the basket from Pressure Pot and drain the water.

13. In the Pressure Pot, place oil and press "Sauté". Now add the scotch eggs and garlic and cook for about 3-4 minutes or until golden brown from all sides.

14. Transfer scotch eggs onto a plate.

15. Arrange a steamer trivet in the Pressure Pot and pour 1 cup of water.

16. Place the scotch eggs on top of trivet.

17. Close the lid and place the pressure valve to "Seal" position.

18.Press "Manual" and cook under "High Pressure" for

about 6 minutes.

19.Press "Cancel" and carefully allow a "Quick" release.

20. Open the lid and serve immediately.

21. Nutrition info: Per serving: Calories: 345, Fats: 22g,

Carbs: 0.4g, Sugar: 0.4g, Proteins: 36g, Sodium:

224mg

Garlic and Herb Carrots

Servings: 3

Cooking Time: 18 Minutes

Ingredients:

• 2 tbsps. butter

• 1 lb. baby carrots

• 1 cup water

• 1 tsp. fresh thyme or oregano

• 1 tsp. minced garlic

• Black pepper

• Coarse Sea salt

Directions:

1. Add water to the inner pot of the Pressure Pot, and then put in a steamer basket.

2. Layer the carrots into the steamer basket.

3. Close and seal the lid, with the pressure vent in the "Sealing" position.

4. Select the "Steam" setting and cook for 2 minutes on high pressure.

5. Quick release the pressure and then carefully remove the steamer basket with the steamed carrots, discarding the water.

6. Add butter to the inner pot of the Pressure Pot and allow it to melt on the "Sauté" function.

7. Add garlic and sauté for 30 seconds, and then add the carrots. Mix well.

8. Stir in the fresh herbs and cook for 2-3 minutes.

9. Season with salt and black pepper, and the transfer to a serving bowl.

10. Serve warm and enjoy!

11. Nutrition info: Calories 122, Carbs 12g, Fat 7 g, Protein 1 g, Potassium (K) 358 mg, Sodium (Na) 189 mg

Bread and Butter Pudding

Servings: 2

Cooking Time: 20 Minutes

Ingredients:

- 1 cup single cream
- 1 large egg
- 2 slices stale bread
- 1tbsp brown sugar
- 1tsp salted butter

Directions:

1. Whisk together the egg, cream, and sugar.

2. Butter the bread and layer it in a small heat-proof bowl.

3. Pour the egg mix over the bread. Pour a cup of water into the Pressure Pot.

4. Place the bowl in the steamer basket and the basket in the Pressure Pot.

5. Cook on Steam, low pressure, for 20 minutes.

6. Depressurize quickly and serve.

7. Nutrition info: Per serving: Calories: 560;Carbs: 40 ;Sugar: 29 ;Fat: 40 ;Protein: 9 ;GL: 30

Stuffed Apples

Servings: 2

Cooking Time: 20 Minutes

Ingredients:

• 2 medium cooking apples

• 2oz blackberries

• 2tbsp honey

• 1/2tsp cinnamon

Directions:

1. Core the apples, leaving a little at the base for structure.

2. Mix the honey, cinnamon, and blackberries, and pack into the apples.

3. Place the apples in the steamer basket in your Pressure Pot.

4. Pour a cup of water into your Pressure Pot.

5. Seal and cook on Steam 20 minutes.

6. Depressurize naturally.

7. Nutrition info: Per serving: Calories: 129;Carbs: 31 ;Sugar: 15 ;Fat: 0 ;Protein: 1 ;GL: 16

Lightning Source UK Ltd.
Milton Keynes UK
UKHW021443200721
387459UK00004B/37